WHERE DID JESUS GO?

TOMMY MANN

WESTBOW
PRESS
A DIVISION OF THOMAS NELSON

WestBow Press books may be ordered through booksellers or by contacting:

WestBow Press
A Division of Thomas Nelson
1663 Liberty Drive
Bloomington, IN 47403
www.westbowpress.com
1 (866) 928-1240

Because of the dynamic nature of the Internet, any web addresses or links contained in this book may have changed since publication and may no longer be valid. The views expressed in this work are solely those of the author and do not necessarily reflect the views of the publisher, and the publisher hereby disclaims any responsibility for them.

Any people depicted in stock imagery provided by Thinkstock are models, and such images are being used for illustrative purposes only. Certain stock imagery © Thinkstock.

ISBN: 978-1-4908-1690-6 (sc)
ISBN: 978-1-4908-1691-3 (e)

Library of Congress Control Number: 2013921436

Printed in the United States of America.

WestBow Press rev. date: 12/05/2013

To my Mom:

From miles away I still feel
your love and support. Thanks for all
you have done for me. I love you!

CONTENTS

CHAPTER 1

❦

WHERE DID JESUS GO?

Where did Jesus go? This is a question that many people wonder about. After His death on the cross the body of Jesus remained in a tomb, but the soul of Jesus had to go somewhere. So where did Jesus go? Where did He spend the time between Good Friday and Easter Sunday?

Many people believe that Jesus naturally went up to heaven; after all, if anybody deserved to go to heaven after death it would be the sinless Son of God. And after all that He went through on the cross to please the Father one would think that heaven would be His immediate reward.

Others believe that the soul of Jesus descended into hell; in order to truly defeat death and hell would He not have to go down there and do battle with the evil one? Christian theology teaches that Jesus was the substitute for the sins of the world, and since humanity deserves hell because of its sin, would not a substitute have to face hell in our place?

People who adhere to these two theories use Bible verses to back up their beliefs. Naturally they cannot both be right, despite the fact that they are using the same Bible to form their theology. There also exist some groups that use no Scripture to support their thoughts of where Jesus went.

Perhaps there is some other theory; maybe, some claim, that the soul of Jesus simply remained in the tomb with the body. Maybe angels came and ministered to Him like after His forty-day fast in Matthew 4:11. Maybe Jesus went to purgatory. But these are only theories. They have no Scriptural support, and too many teachers today are leading students astray with their thoughts and opinions instead of what the Holy Spirit has already inspired for us in the Word of God.

This book will look at Scripture to form the conclusion to the question of where Jesus really went, as well as what He did once He got there. There is certainly room for debate on some of these topics, so any personal opinions from the author will be specified as being just that, opinions from my "biblical imagination." Otherwise, all facts will be derived from the very words of Jesus in the gospel accounts, and the very words that God breathed through the holy men of God that served as the human authors of the Bible.

CHAPTER 2

❦

WHERE DO PEOPLE GO?

Before we can look at where Jesus went we have to fully understand where people go. When people die today there are only two options for their soul's eternal destination: heaven and hell. How do we know this? All through its pages the Bible teaches about both heaven and hell. These are undeniable facts in the Word of God. However, one would search the Scriptures in vain looking for a reference to a third option. There is no such word or idea that conveys the thought of a purgatory, a middle ground, an eternal sleep, or just ceasing to exist, as some religions and cults claim (see Chapter 12 for more on purgatory).

Some groups are content to claim that the Bible is their *final* authority, and yet they form their post-mortem theology on periodicals, magazines, or the oral teachings of their leaders. If the Bible is the one and only Word of God then we do not need to read *The Watchtower, The Pearl of Great Price,* or put our eternal stock in the teachings of a man who claims to be the spokesman of God.

The apostle Paul said that if anyone were to present some other gospel than what has already been presented then that person will be cursed (Galatians 1:8-9). He even said that *an angel* might come with another gospel. An angel might come with an extra-biblical message for someone, but that does not mean that the angel is from the Lord, for there are fallen angels who work for Satan. These messengers are to be marked and ignored, and all preachers of the true gospel must call them out by name as Paul did in II Timothy 2:16-18.

We will now return to the question posed at the beginning of this chapter, where do people go? Where do they go when they die?

Most go to hell. I know right away that this is not an encouraging thought, but it is the gospel truth. Jesus Himself said these words: "Enter by the narrow gate. For the gate is wide and the way is easy that leads to destruction, and those who enter by it are many. For the gate is narrow and the way is hard that leads to life, and those who find it are few. (Matthew 7:13-14)."

Jesus said that the path that leads to hell is broad, and that many (compared to few) will walk down that path to their own eternal destruction. Why do so many choose the path bound for hell? First of all, they are born on that path. Every person who has ever lived (with the exception of Jesus Christ) has sinned (Romans 3:23); we are that way by birth. When Adam and Eve first sinned in the Garden of Eden they passed sin on to all of their descendants[1].

God's standard for admittance into heaven is perfection, but none of us will achieve that. The punishment for the imperfect is hell (Romans 6:23). So unless a person can do something about his sin he will never get off of the road headed for destruction.

Many people are on that road because, secondly, they are deceived. Matthew 7:13-14 was just cited, but the next verse in the passage shows that many people are on the broad road because many false prophets come in as wolves in sheep's clothing. These are the preachers that want to have the largest crowd or

---

[1]   This does not negate the age of accountability. For more information on what happens when babies and young children die, please see my book *Asleep in Heaven's Nursery* (Tate Publishing and Enterprises).

4

sell the most books so they say and write what feels good instead of the truth. If this book were all about how to be blessed by God beyond your wildest dreams it would fly off the shelves, but God has called us to present His truth, not to tickle people's itching ears as Paul predicted would happen in the last days (II Timothy 4:3).

There are also wolves in sheep's clothing that do not want to "offend" anyone or "beat them up over their sin." These false prophets create an environment in which lukewarm congregants can come as they are and, because of messages designed to not allow for conviction, leave as they are. This epidemic is causing millions of unsaved, unrepentant people to feel good about their spiritual condition, and therefore never get off the broad road. They are not made to view their sin as offensive to a holy God.

The third reason that many people are on this broad path is that these travelers prefer the journey on the broad road to that of the narrow one. The time spent on the broad road promises fun, entertainment, amusement, security, friends, and a future. This is contrasted with the false advertisement about their counterparts on the narrow road. This path is portrayed as being a road for the dull, boring, goody-goodies, or the narrow-minded hypocrites.

Even if all of this were true, the destination for those on the narrow road is far better than the destination of those on the broad road. The former is eternity in heaven, while the latter is a sentence in hell. Even *if it were true*. But as stated before, this is simply false advertisement.

The Christian life, the *real* Christian life on the narrow road, is not just about denial. Yes, a Christian must deny himself and give up the things of this world, but there is a replacement principle here. When the things of this world are given up for the cause of Christ there will be a replacement with the things of Christ.

Worldly relationships are replaced with godly relationships; sinful music is replaced with uplifting music; things once thought to be fun by the lost person will now seem foolish to the saved person, all the while the Christian lifestyle will become satisfying and enjoyable to him. So in reality, the narrow road is the better choice both in life and after life.

The fourth reason that people will never make a u-turn and divert themselves from the broad road is that they think they are on the narrow road already. These are the people that think they are good enough just by being a good person. This false assumption will probably cause more people to go to hell than any other factor.

The person who thinks that he is good enough on his own only needs to take the good person test to find out. Just like the student who takes a placement test so that his academic level can be properly evaluated, so too the "good person" must take this test to properly evaluate the level of his goodness.

The good person test (taken from The Way of the Master series with Ray Comfort and Kirk Cameron[2]) is quite simple. Since many people generally believe that they will be judged according to how well they kept the Ten Commandments from Exodus 20 in order to make it into heaven, they just need to look at a few of the commandments.

Ask a person if they have ever lied, stolen anything (regardless of value), or looked at someone with lust. This is just 30% of the Ten Commandments.

If the person answers honestly then he will have to admit that he is a lying, thieving, adulterer who has to face God on judgment day. Plus the Bible tells us that even if we had only broken one part of God's law we are still guilty of all the law (James 2:10). Suddenly the good person does not seem so good anymore.

Until people realize that they are not good enough to switch roads they will forever stay on the broad one. It is essential for these folks to understand that only Jesus can move them from the road that is broad to the road that is narrow.

---

[2]   www.wayofthemaster.com

The point has been made that when people die they will either go to heaven or hell, and that most will end up in hell. The same passage from Matthew 17 that reveals that many will follow the wide path to destruction also reveals that only a few will make the switch to the narrow road that leads to heaven.

What about you? Where will you go? The purpose of this book is to teach on the topic of where Jesus spent the time between Good Friday and Easter Sunday, but knowledge of the Bible will profit a man nothing if he is not a believer himself. Too many people today think they have been born again because they know Bible trivia, but on judgment day that trivia will not save a soul.

So have you made the switch from the broad road to the narrow road? If you have never made that u-turn, if you have never been changed from the inside out, then please do not move on to the next chapter until you have given your life to the Lord. Chapter Three will still be here after you talk to the Lord. If this is for you, will you pray now and ask the Lord to forgive you for your sins and to save you? Then repent, get off at the nearest exit, and get on the narrow heaven-bound road.

CHAPTER 3

❦

JESUS DID NOT GO
TO HEAVEN

Yes, I said it.

One of the greatest misconceptions of our time is that Jesus went back to heaven after His death on the cross. Since this is such a popular theory I realize that even the title of this chapter may have some people upset. The thought of Jesus not going to heaven even sounds a little blasphemous, but we cannot make the Bible say something that it does not say just to make ourselves feel better.

The first proof that Jesus did not go up to heaven on Good Friday is the most obvious point—the Bible never says that He did. Of course there are some things not expressly written in the Word of God, like the words rapture, trinity, or age of accountability, that are still biblical concepts. And the idea of a Christian, especially Jesus, going to heaven after death is certainly a biblical concept, but there are other things which are expressly written in the Word of God which teach something totally different.

Aside from the fact that the Bible never tells its readers that Jesus spent this time in heaven is another undeniable fact: the Bible tells its readers that He did *not* spend this time in heaven. In fact, Jesus Himself introduces this idea. Consider the very words of the recently resurrected Rabbi in John 20:16-17: "Jesus said to her, 'Mary.' She turned and said to him in Aramaic, 'Rabboni!' (which means Teacher)" "She must have flung her arms around Him, perhaps embracing His feet in keeping with the custom of that day[3]."

"Jesus said to her, 'Do not cling to me, for *I have not yet ascended to the Father...* (italics mine)'"

There on Easter morning Mary Magdalene encountered Jesus in bodily form. One gets the impression that Mary is overjoyed at the sight of her living Master and she rushes towards Him for an embrace. It must have pained Jesus to stop her in her tracks, but as He made clear, He had not yet ascended up to His Father. To put this in other words, Jesus hadn't been to heaven yet.

The verse continues with Jesus telling Mary to go tell the disciples that Jesus is going to ascend to His Father, so the reader must conclude that after Jesus' mission was accomplished He went home to spend some time with God.

Some Bible scholars believe that Jesus did not want Mary to act the same way towards Him as she had in the past. They believe that the pre-resurrection familiarity should be done away with now that His mission was over. Others believe that Jesus simply wanted His Father to be the first to comfort Him and rejoice with Him after the horrendous crucifixion. But perhaps the best explanation for this is the fact that Jesus did not have a glorified body yet.

Obviously the body that Mary saw was not identical to the one that had hung on Calvary's cross just days before; that body was not even recognizable as belonging to a human. Since Mary originally thought that the Man who spoke to her in the garden was just someone tending to the garden and not her mangled Savior, one might conclude that Jesus' body was not glorified, but at least healed to some degree. Others could argue that Mary was

---

[3]   Cross, John R. *By This Name*, GoodSeed International p.297

delusional with grief, she didn't get a good look at Him, or it was simply too dark that early in the morning for her to recognize the figure of the One she was talking to. Whichever the case, the point is that Jesus was not sporting a glorified body.

Some people will argue that Jesus *must* have gone to heaven, for, as we all know, to be absent from the body is to be present with the Lord. The problem is that verse does not appear in the Bible. The verse that most Christians often misquote is II Corinthians 5:8, which says: "We are confident, I say, and willing rather to be absent from the body, and to be present with the Lord."

The difference is verbally small but theologically large. Paul is not saying "to be absent is to be present." In fact, what Paul was really trying to say is, "I would rather be with the Lord than be here in this body." But Paul was not teaching a theological truth that says "to be absent is to be present" but "I would rather be absent here and present there."

Don't get me wrong. I firmly believe that when a person dies they immediately face the Lord as their judge, and those who were saved on earth will enter into the presence of the Lord. But if we make this verse say something it was not trying to say then we get in a situation where Jesus *had* to be in heaven or else the Bible is wrong. That is why a person must properly discern the Word of God in order to avoid error or contradiction. It is this same error in interpretation that leads to the next chapter.

CHAPTER 4

❦

JESUS DID NOT
GO TO HELL

There are a lot of people that think that Jesus spent the time between Good Friday and Easter Sunday in hell. After all, if Jesus had to defeat death and be a substitute for our sins then He needed to go all the way to hell to do it.

One of the verses that is used to support this theory is found in Ephesians 4:8-10: "Therefore it says, 'When he ascended on high he led a host of captives, and he gave gifts to men.' (In saying, 'He ascended,' what does it mean but that he had also descended into the lower regions, the earth? He who descended is the one who also ascended far above all the heavens, that he might fill all things.)"

This passage is clearly talking about Jesus. Not only did Jesus ascend up far above the heavens, but these verses point out that Jesus also descended into the lower parts of the earth. This is their definitive evidence that Jesus went to hell, but is that really where Jesus descended?

Acts 2:31 says that Jesus' soul "was not left in hell." This also seems to make the case that Jesus was in hell. Another verse that makes a similar assertion is Matthew 12:40: "For as Jonah was three days and three nights in the whale's belly, so shall the Son of Man be three days and three nights in the heart of the earth."

The Son of Man is without a doubt Jesus Christ. This was a title of humility that showed that He was not just the Son of God, but was 100% man as He walked on the earth. Jesus referred to Himself as the Son of Man on many occasions, thirty-two of which are found in the book of Matthew alone.

The book of Jonah in the Old Testament tells of the prophet who refused to obey the instructions of God and fled on a ship heading the opposite way from where God told him to go. The Lord caused a great storm to plague the ship, and the crew believed that Jonah had angered the gods, so he was cast overboard. The Lord prepared a large fish to swallow his wayward prophet, and for three days he sat among the whale's lunch and digestive juices until he was vomited up on dry ground.

So in Matthew 12:40 Jesus predicted that just as Jonah had been in the belly of the fish for three days, so He too would be in the "heart of the earth" for three days. This caps off a list of verses that seemingly, without question, prove that Jesus went to hell.

He definitely descended, He went to the center of the earth, and His soul "was not left in hell." Is there some other place Jesus could have gone that would allow all three of these statements to be correct without Jesus burning in hell? I believe there is, but before we go there we have to first tackle another question. Did Jesus have to go to hell in order to properly be our substitute?

In theological circles we often speak of the substitutionary atonement. This is the idea that Jesus' death on the cross made us able to have fellowship with Him (atonement), and that He took our place (substitution). Two illustrations can help a person understand both words a little better. First consider the word atonement.

To atone is to make amends. A good way to remember this word is to divide it in half. Turn atone into "at one." When two people have been involved in some sort of dispute, then they make up and forgive each other, they become "at one" with each other.

We were all born at odds with God, not at one with Him. To make matters worse, we were so far gone that there was nothing we could do to make amends. This is why God offered His one and only Son as an offering to make amends with us. After God did His part two thousand years ago the ball is now in our court. God has done everything He can to restore the relationship, and now it is totally up to us to complete the work of atonement by denying ourselves and entering into a relationship with Him.

The work of atonement was God's part. He offered His Son for us. The work of substitution, however, was done by the Son. Jesus substituted Himself for us to please the Father.

Consider a courtroom scene. You are the defendant and you have just been found guilty of a heinous crime. Satan is the prosecutor, God is the Judge, and you have no defense. As Satan makes his closing remarks and reminds the honorable Judge of all your many offenses, he glares right at you and asks the court for what he really wants: the death penalty.

A judge only has one job to do in this case, and that is to punish the crime. He may be a nice guy, a loving husband, a volunteer firefighter, and involved in every local charity, but he still has to punish every crime. Anything less would make him unjust.

The same is true of God. Yes, He is kind, faithful, patient, forgiving, and loving. But He is also just, and He must punish the crime. The prosecutor, whom the Bible calls the accuser of Christians (Revelation 12:10), is right—we are guilty and deserving death and hell. God, whom the Bible calls the judge of all the earth (Genesis 18:25), must sentence us accordingly.

But just as the gavel comes down in the courtroom the back door swings open, and Jesus asks for permission to approach the bench. "Your Honor," He begins, "the defendant is guilty. But I want you to punish me instead." This act makes it possible for the Judge to punish the crime while letting the actual criminal go free. This is how Jesus served as our substitute.

Before going on it must be noted that even though Jesus has already taken our place, we must still do something about it. Jesus offers us a free gift, but just like with any gift, we have to reach out and receive it.

You can stare at a Christmas present forever; that doesn't make it yours. You can look at it, believe it's there, and even be thankful for it, but it does you no good until you reach out and take the gift.

The same is true with our salvation. It is not enough to believe Jesus became our substitute—the demons in hell believe this, and they tremble with fear (James 2:19). Our belief must lead us to do something, to wit, we must change our lives and follow Jesus as His servants.

So Jesus became our substitute by shedding His innocent blood and dying for us. This means that Jesus did not have to experience the flames of hell fire in order to fully take our place. According to Romans 6:23 the punishment for our sins is death. Hell is a place of punishment for those who rejected God during their life, and we know that Jesus never rejected His Father. And Jesus did not have to go to hell.

Did everyone in hell reject God?

It is this author's opinion that everyone in hell rejected God. This is not to say that everyone in hell chose some religion or cult over Christianity. In fact, hell is full of good people. Jesus told us in Matthew 7:22-23 that hell will be full of preachers, teachers, and other godly people. So how did they reject God?

People reject God by not surrendering 100% of their lives to Him. To surrender 99% is to make yourself a god. The rich young ruler of Matthew 19 rejected God even though he claimed to have obeyed all the commandments of the Mosaic Law, but as Jesus pointed out in verses 20-21, there was still one thing that he lacked. Christ demands 100% obedience to His words.

That is not to say that we have to become sinless in order to be saved. But it does mean that we should live like we want to become sinless. As a basketball player I never yelled back at my coach and said, "God doesn't expect me to be perfect so neither should you!" No, I always pushed myself and tried to get as close to perfection as possible. In the Christian life we should try just as hard to get as close to perfection as possible.

Even people who have never been to church or heard of Jesus can still experience His salvation. The Bible tells us that the heavens declare that there is a God (Psalm 19:1) and that He is righteous (Psalm 97:6). Any person should be able to look around and realize that there had to have been some divine Creator that shaped this world, and that we are not the result of some accident or random chance. If there is a Creator than He must be a God, and I believe that in the Sovereignty of God this acknowledgement can lead a person into a saving knowledge of Christ.

A lot of Christians like to debate whether or not a man who was born on a deserted island and grew up all alone would go to hell when he dies. Although it is pointless for Christians to waste time debating useless hypothetical situations (how did he get on the island?), I believe that God will reveal Himself to this man if he comes to the realization that there must be a God and desires to find Him. Since Hebrews 11:6 says that God rewards those who diligently seek Him then God would somehow reveal himself to this man.

We were all born with God's law written on our hearts, and something deep within each of us knows that there is a God out there. Some shrug off that feeling; others drown it in alcohol, drugs, and pleasure; others pursue it, God meets them, and they are saved.

But if the man on the island were to acknowledge that some higher power must have created the world around him, yet not care to find out just who this Being might be, he is rejecting God and sentencing himself to hell.

Here is the point of all of this: people only go to hell for dying without surrendering their lives to God. We do not need a substitute to take our place on this issue, we just need to surrender! Jesus' death satisfied the sin problem, which allows us to have the freedom to submit our lives to God; if we do not do this we go to hell, but Jesus did not have to go to hell to give us this freedom, He just had to die and shed His perfect blood.

For whatever reason, shedding blood has always been God's way of atonement. When Adam and Eve committed the first sin in the Garden of Eden their eyes were opened and they realized they were naked. They used fig leaves (which are sharp and no doubt uncomfortable) to make clothes for themselves. Do you remember what God did to better clothe them? He made them clothes from animal skins. I'm not a taxidermist, but I do know that you cannot skin an animal without killing it and shedding its blood (Genesis 3).

All through the Old Testament God continued to require bloodshed and the death of an animal to make temporary atonement with His children. Before a sacrifice each person would place his hands on the head of the lamb, symbolically transferring his sin to the lamb, and the lamb's throat was slit (which is the most painless way to kill a lamb).

That system continued for 2,000 years, and one day a man named John the Baptist saw his cousin Jesus coming, and he yelled, "Behold, the Lamb of God that takes away the sins of the world (John 1:29)!" Just as each person would transfer his sin to the lamb (who was required to be without spot or defect and thus symbolically pure), so Jesus, "who knew no sin, became sin for us (II Corinthians 5:21)" when He died on the cross. God was satisfied to place all of our sins on this spotless Lamb as a final sacrifice for sin.

Therefore, Jesus did not have to face hell to be our substitute. He only needed to be perfect and shed His blood for us. Hell was never created for people anyway, so Jesus would not have to defeat it. Hell was not part of God's original plan, and was a place He created after Lucifer rebelled and took a host of angels with him (Matthew 25:41).

But there were three verses mentioned earlier in this chapter that seemingly make the case that Jesus did go to hell (His soul was not left in hell, he descended into the lower parts of the earth, and He spent three days and three nights in the heart of the earth). How can we reconcile the difference? It's easy.

Jesus *did* go to hell.

Kind of.

Just not the hell you might be thinking of.

Just turn the page. I'll explain in the next chapter.

CHAPTER 5

❦

A DIFFERENT KIND OF HELL

Have you ever gotten confused with some of the different words the Bible uses for things? With words such as hell, lake of fire, Hades, Gahenna, heaven, New Jerusalem, and paradise all floating around in the New Testament it can be easy to lose track of which place is being described.

Some people think all those words are only describing two places. Hell, Hades, and the lake of fire are all synonyms for the place bad people go, while heaven, paradise, and the New Jerusalem are interchangeable terms for the eternal dwelling place of the saved. That is just not the case, however. Hopefully this chapter will help to shine some light on the differences between them.

Many times as Christians we make the mistake of referring to hell as the place of eternal punishment for those who reject God (I did in the last chapter, but I was building up to this point). As pastors we can really throw a clincher into the invitation by telling the congregation, "If you don't accept Christ today you could die and spend eternity in hell."

The truth is *no one* will spend eternity in hell.

Before you call me a heretic hear me out. The lost will spend eternity in the lake of fire, not hell. The difference between the two is the same as the difference between prison and jail. Jail is a holding cell where people are initially booked and wait for their trial. Those who are convicted and sentenced to a term of more than a year (in most cases) are moved to prison.

Those who die today without Christ go to hell to await their final judgment at the Great White Throne (Revelation 20:11-12). After they are found guilty they will be sent to their eternal place of punishment, which is a lake of fire. Consider Revelation 20:14-15: "And death and hell were cast into the lake of fire. This is the second death. And whosoever was not found written in the Book of Life was cast into the lake of fire."

Everyone in hell and hell itself will be cast into the lake of fire. Is this lake really permanent? The tenth verse of the same chapter tells us that Satan will be cast into the lake, and they "shall be tormented day and night, forever and ever."

Recently a well-known preacher wrote a book where he questions the validity of a literal hell. He made the statement that if there were a God who would torture people in hell for eternity, then that God should be rejected. It is interesting how he left these verses from Revelation out of his book.

So no one is in the lake of fire today, and hell is populated with those who have rejected Christ since the beginning of creation. But what about Hades? What is this place, and who is there now?

For those who only read the King James Version of the Bible you will never see this word appear in your Bible. The New King James Version and the subsequent newer translations use the word Hades many times throughout their pages.

Hades is a Greek word that refers to the ancient god of the underworld of mythology. Before this mythology came about Jesus used the word to describe the real underworld. In Luke 16:23 we see the story of the rich man and Lazarus. After the death of the rich man the Bible tells us that he lifted up his eyes in hell (Hades). Since this story was an actual event we learn that Hades is an actual place.

We also learn from this passage that Hades is a place of punishment by fire for those who rejected Christ (i.e. the rich man). The rich man also acknowledged the fact that his brothers would share the same fate if they did not repent and change their lives. We will come back to this passage again later.

Is Luke 16 a parable or a real event?

There are many Bible scholars who believe and teach that the events of Luke 16:19-31 are not factual, but comprise another parable of Jesus. A good way to define a parable is "an earthly story with a heavenly meaning." A more professional definition would be "an extended simile."

An earthly story with a heavenly meaning would be a story told about earthly things used to make a spiritual application. This is like what many preachers and teachers do today. A simile is a comparison using the words "like" or "as" (this is similar to a metaphor, but a metaphor *does not* use like or as).

An example of a simile would be, "It's as cold as ice in here." An extended simile would employ an entire story after the word *as*. "It's as cold as that time we went to Antarctica and we..." Each of the parables that Jesus used were extended similes.

Jesus often used parables to help His listeners understand what He was trying to teach. Most of the parables of Jesus began with "the kingdom of heaven is like..." or "the kingdom of heaven is as..." The former can be found six times in Matthew 13 alone.

The reason this has been pointed out is there is no simile found in Luke 16. In fact, in verse nineteen where this passage begins Jesus said, "There *was* a certain rich man (italics mine). Jesus did not use this event to paint a picture; He was telling an actual story to teach us some doctrinal truth.

Also, the parables of the Bible do not record any names, but Luke 16 specifically mentions Lazarus (not the one Jesus raised from the dead in John 11:43) and Abraham, whom everyone knows was an actual character from history.

Luke 16:19-31 was an actual event, not a parable. This is so important to understand because Luke 16 is the key that unlocks a lot of the mystery that surrounds the concept of Hades. The fact that liberal theologians have tried to push this story off as a parable serves as a reminder that in the last days people will try to erase the concept of hell from the pages of holy writ. No matter how many of these false prophets attempt to undermine God's Word, always stick to what God's Words actually says.

We now see that Hades is a real place. So to go back to the question that this book set out to answer, the question of where did Jesus go, I believe that Jesus went to Hades.

Hades

It is imperative that we do not mix up hell and Hades. Many people use the words interchangeably, but they are not one in the same. If a person were to look up a passage in both the King James Bible and the New King James Bible they might think that both words refer to the same place (Revelation 1:18, for example), but they are different. The KJV uses the word hell to refer to both hell and Hades, while newer translations make the distinction between the two. We will see why they are both accurate shortly.

There are three parts to Hades, one of which is hell. Hell is a very real place inside of another real place called Hades. This hell is everything that we know hell to be—a place of torment, fire, weeping and wailing, darkness, and sheer terror, reserved for those who die having rejected Jesus while on earth.

I am a native Floridian, having grown up in Orlando. Today I live in Union, South Carolina. If I were to take a trip back to my home city I could make two statements, both of which would be correct. I could say, "I am going to Orlando next week," or I could say, "I am going to Florida next week." While one is a little more specific, both are true. This is how there is no discrepancy between the KJV and the newer translations on this issue. When the King James Version says someone went to hell while the New King James Version says the same man went to Hades, they are both correct. The former is just being more specific than the latter.

Hell, the place of torment, is the first part of Hades. The second part is Paradise, the place of comfort. It is amazing how these two places that are polar opposites can both exist in one place, but they do. Paradise is also known as Abraham's bosom (Luke 16:22). The title of this book is *Where Did Jesus Go?* The answer is, He went to Hades. But to be more specific, He went to Paradise.

Remember the thief on the cross next to Jesus? There were actually two, but only one chose to place his trust in Jesus. In Luke 23 we read about a man being executed for the crimes he committed (which were probably far more than mere thievery), and just before his death he chose to mock Jesus, who was being executed next to him. The other thief acknowledged that he was getting what he deserved, but he confessed that Jesus had done nothing wrong. Then he turned to Jesus and prayed a prayer that saved his soul, "Lord, remember me when you come into your kingdom (Luke 23:42)."

The answer that Jesus gave this thief is often quoted but seldom understood properly. In the next verse Jesus said, "Today shalt thou be with me in Paradise." Many people just casually pass this off as assuming that Jesus was using a descriptive word for heaven, but in actuality He was speaking of the literal place where they would both be in a matter of hours.

Hell is one part of Hades, Paradise is another part, but there is still a third part. There is a great gulf between the other two places. In Luke 16 the rich man could see Abraham far off, so he cried out to him to send Lazarus to dip his finger in water and let it drip on his tongue since he was tormented in flames. Picking

Lazarus was an odd choice since the Bible tells us that Lazarus was a poor beggar that sat outside the gates of the rich man and begged for food every day. The rich man never obliged, giving his scraps to the dogs instead.

But Abraham's answer to the rich man was that Lazarus could not perform this task because of the great gulf that was between them. Abraham said that no one could pass from hell to Paradise, or from Paradise to hell due to the gulf. The Greek word used for gulf here is *chasma,* where we get our English word chasm. It means "a gaping opening."

Although that is the clearest picture of the great gulf that we get from Scripture we do know that there is some kind of opening, some gap between hell and Paradise that is impenetrable. The people in hell cannot do anything about their plight, even if the ones in Paradise wanted to help them.

There are several things that we can learn from the story in Luke 16 about what life in Hades is like. People in Hades have:

> *Eyes—"in hell he lifted up his eyes...v.23"*
> *Fingers—"dip the tip of his finger in water...v.24"*
> *Tongue—"cool my tongue...v.24"*
> *Feeling—"I am tormented...v.24"*
> *Memory—"Remember...v.25"*
> *Awareness—"I have five brethren...v.28"*

This is significant. We see that people in Paradise have all their faculties. They are being comforted in the company of all the saints that have gone on before. Besides this they are able to enjoy a perfect life as they are rewarded for having given their lives to God.

In Luke 16 we read about both Lazarus and Abraham being in Paradise together. Abraham's life story is recorded all the way back in the book of Genesis. It is astounding to think about thousands of years of believers all living in the same place.

But if we are going to look at the good part of the afterlife we have to be fair and look at the bad part as well. People in hell do not simply just cease to be; they have all their senses accounted for as they experience indescribable agony.

I will admit that there are some who disagree here that people will be tormented in hell forever. There are three popular schools of thought when it comes to this part of Hades: there are those with a literal view, those with a symbolic view, and those who are annihilationists. Literalists, like this author, take the Bible literally and believe that the imagery Jesus used to describe the flames of hell are exactly what He meant. Those who hold to the symbolic interpretation think that Jesus was simply painting a picture about how terrible that fate would be.

Those who subscribe to the concept of annihilation think that perhaps flames will burn forever and ever, but the unregenerate will be consumed and destroyed, not suffering for all eternity. However, this annihilation could not occur until the dead are cast into the lake of fire; even the annihilationist must concede that people are being tormented in Hades today.

So whether a person is a literalist, symbolist, or annihilationist, one thing is clear: Hades is a terrible place. Max Anders, general editor of the Holman Bible Commentary, wrote in his book *What You Need to Know About Bible Prophecy* that, "The truth behind the horrible imagery is that hell is a place of profound misery where the unsaved are separated from the presence of God forever[4]."

This shows us that people cannot claim a symbolic view simply because the flames of hell are not in keeping with a loving, merciful God. I have heard too many people say that Jesus was just painting a picture by referring to flames, and that His character would not allow Hades to be like that. But if that is the case, then even if Jesus were making a point, His point is that Hades is

---

4   Anders, Max, *What You Need to Know About Bible Prophecy,* Thomas Nelson Publishers, p.136

awful. Imagery is only good if it paints an accurate picture. Even a loving, merciful God allows people to go to Hades because He is equally a just God. As Christians we need to alert the lost world of the seriousness of this dreadful fate.

I know some people are thinking, "People can't get saved just because they don't want to go to hell." That is true, but it is hard to get saved if they don't *know* there is a hell. Hell represents the judgment of God, the fact that He hates sin and cannot allow it to go unpunished. Sinners see no need to repent when the pastor gives a talk about how much God wants to bless everyone.

In hell there are also thousands of years, hundreds of generations of people all living together. Unlike the ones in Paradise, these aren't the saints that will serve as their roommates; these are some of the worst people one could imagine. I believe that hell is full of good people, the ones who lived good lives, the ones who even thought that they were saved, but who did not fully submit themselves to the Lordship of Jesus Christ. These are the people described by Jesus in Matthew 7:22-23:

> "Many will say to me in that day, 'Lord, Lord, have we not prophesied in your name? And in your name have cast out devils? And in your name have done many wonderful works?' And then will I profess unto them, 'I never knew you. Depart from me, you that work iniquity.'"

It is terribly sad to think that so many good people, people who taught Sunday school classes, drove church buses, gave money, went on missions trips, and sang in the choir, will go to hell because they work iniquity (or "practice lawlessness"). Not only will they miss spending eternity with Jesus, and not only will they go to hell, but they will also live among the evil people who chose hell out of hatred for God. These same good people will be in hell with people we see in the Bible like Goliath, the residents of Sodom, Queen Jezebel, and Haman. There will also be people not recorded in the Bible like Adolf Hitler, the 9/11 hijackers, Sadaam Hussein, and Emperor Nero.

We have already discussed in this chapter how hell is not permanent, but the lake of fire is. Just because hell will one day be destroyed does not mean that the punishment will go away.

Hell will not last forever.

Neither will Paradise.

CHAPTER 6

PARADISE

I recently heard a popular pastor preach about heaven. We were at a county-wide revival so there were a lot of members of our church there. The sermon was very good, as all sermons on heaven usually are, but there was one part of the message that I didn't quite agree with.

The pastor used the quote from Jesus to the thief on the cross that we have already discussed: today shalt thou be with me in Paradise. The pastor went on to talk about how Jesus described heaven as being a place of paradise.

Ordinarily in a situation like that I would be inclined to keep a discrepancy like that to myself. As long as he is preaching the gospel message of Jesus Christ we are okay; we can disagree on a few things. I hate to hear of Christians breaking fellowship over matters of music style, drums in the church, eschatology, or the necessity of ties. We are going to disagree on some things, but as long as we love Jesus and teach His truth we are on the same team.

But just a few weeks prior to this revival service I had preached in our church about Paradise, and I had used the Scripture to show that Paradise isn't heaven. Because of that I had some people from our church ask me which one of us was correct. Without trying to sound cocky I had to remind them that I backed up my beliefs with the Bible while the other person just made a generalization.

I referred to that event as a reminder that it is easy to make assumptions about things in the Bible, and that each Christian must make sure that he carefully interprets God's Word. This is why Paul told Timothy to study hard and be "rightly dividing the Word of truth (II Timothy 2:15)." Just because something in the Bible sounds biblical doesn't mean that it is truth.

Heaven is paradise, and Paradise is heavenly, but they are not the same place.

Just as hell is like a holding cell within Hades, so Paradise is also like a holding cell. There is an important difference between the two cells though. We read in Luke 16 that the rich man in hell was suffering in torment because he was in a cell of punishment. But what we read about Lazarus in his cell is much different. In Luke 16:25 Abraham told the rich man that Lazarus was being "comforted."

Paradise was not a cell of punishment; it was a place of rest and comfort. We see that the rich man is crying out in pain and despair, but Abraham is able to talk back to him under control. There is no reason to believe from this passage that Abraham is in any way uncomfortable where he is.

So a natural question may now arise: why would God send these believers to a holding cell? These are the good ones, right? These are the people who, according to Hebrews 11:13, "died in faith, not having received the promises, but having seen them afar off, and were persuaded of them, and embraced them…" So why would God make them sit for up to 4,000 years in a holding cell?

The answer is really quite obvious: these people could not go to heaven because of their sin. Under the Old Covenant the best that people could do was delay God's judgment of their sin, but their sin could not be forgiven. God is very much a loving, forgiving God, but He is just as much holy and just as He is loving and forgiving. This means that God must punish sin, and according to Romans 6:23, the punishment, or earned payment for sin, is death.

This does not mean that the death of the Old Testament saints satisfied the sin problem, for it is not just a physical death that comes from sin. Revelation 20:14 speaks of a second death, which is the final fate of those who reject Jesus with their lives, and this second death is in the lake of fire (Revelation 2:11, 20:6, and 21:8 also speak of the second death).

So the earned payment for our sins is death and eternal separation from God, and since God is both holy and just, He must see to it that our sentence is carried out. If God were to offer forgiveness to sinners deserving of death, then He would immediately cease to be holy or just. Because of that, Adam and Eve all the way down to the thief on the cross next to Jesus could not go to heaven.

During their lifetime, if they were righteous and "believed in the promises," then they could have God's wrath delayed on them. This concept, known theologically as propitiation, came about as the result of the sacrificial system. When their hands were placed on the lamb's head and their sin was symbolically transferred to the lamb, God's wrath was delayed, meaning that even though they will still face physical death for their sin, God would delay His judgment on the second (spiritual) death.

In Chapter 4 we saw that Jesus was the Lamb of God who took away the sins of the world. Upon the death of Jesus, when the sin of the world was transferred to the spotless Lamb, a final sacrifice was made. God became satisfied to look at the sacrifice of His Son and accept that as our offering. No longer would we need to delay God's wrath through propitiation; Jesus received the full brunt of God's wrath for us. That put God in a position to be able to forgive us while still being just.

The crime has been punished by the Judge! God is still holy and just, and now justified in offering love and forgiveness to the criminals. More than that, God can now rightfully have a relationship with us and still be holy Himself. Our physical death will still come—that is part of the curse of sin—but we will no longer have to face a second death because God is justified in allowing us to live with Him in heaven after our physical death. Jesus became our propitiation (Romans 3:25, I John 2:2, 4:10)!

Under the Old Covenant people became right with God the same way that we do today. Hebrews 11 says that these saints were persuaded of, embraced, and confessed the promises of the coming Messiah. Today we must be persuaded of, embrace, and confess the risen Messiah.

The Keys

Before Jesus' mission was complete, did He need to take the keys from the devil? I heard a really great sermon one time by a great Bible teacher about how Jesus defeated Satan, and then in a further act of humiliation, He took the keys of death and hell from him. I've also seen trembling Satan characters in church plays surrender the keys to a resurrected Jesus. In a movie called *The Apostle*, Robert Duvall delivers an old-fashioned fiery sermon about how "The Holy Ghost went down to hell and did a backflip on the devil" before He took the keys.

Those images can give a Christian goose bumps, but are they accurate? In Revelation 1:18 Jesus introduces Himself as "He that lives and was dead, and behold, I am alive forevermore, Amen; and have the keys of death and hell."

Jesus never said He had to take those keys from the devil, but simply that He had them. Furthermore, the Bible never says that this was part of His mission. The only other keys that Jesus ever speaks of was when He told Peter that He would give him the keys of the kingdom of heaven (Matthew 16:19). These keys should not be thought of as being literal, but as one commentator noted, "keys are a symbol for the authority that Jesus shares with his church." So again, this shows that the power originates from God's throne room, not something that had to be wrestled away from the evil one.[5]

---

[5] *Bible Studies for Texas: The Gospel of Matthew,* BaptistWay Press, p.153

Are we really supposed to think that there are literal keys that unlock heaven and hell? And what would the key to death unlock? And if Jesus had to go to Hades to take those keys from Satan, how long did Satan have them, and how did he get them in the first place? Was Satan in charge of death while he had the keys?

The best way to understand these passages is that the keys are symbolic of authority. When the mayor gives a celebrity the keys to the city, is that key literally a giant master key that will allow him to freely enter any residence or business? Of course not.

Jesus doesn't have a key chain with keys to heaven, hell, and death on it. Rather, as the sovereign ruler of the world, Jesus possesses all authority in these realms.

If Jesus didn't go to Paradise to meet up with the devil and reclaim the keys, then what did He do while He was down there? I Peter 3:19 says that Jesus "preached unto the spirits in prison" while He was down there. But what did He preach? Did these spirits in prison have another chance to repent and be saved?

The word used for preached in this verse is different than the word that is used to preach salvation (consider Luke 16:16 for example; here the word for preached is where we get the word evangelize). The word used for preached here means to herald, publish, or proclaim. So Jesus didn't go down and evangelize the lost; He was proclaiming something. And these spirits in prison are the souls of the believers in Paradise, which we have already seen was a holding cell.

Remember, these were the people who died having not yet seen the promises, but they embraced them. Now, after all these years, the Promised Messiah enters Paradise, and He meets the description of the mangled sacrifice of Isaiah 53. He comes in at long last, and He begins to proclaim Himself, that His mission was accomplished, and that He would be leading these captives to the Father (Ephesians 4:8-10).

31

Way back in Genesis 3:15 humanity was promised a Messiah, and this preaching from Jesus to the spirits was where "Christ proclaimed His victory to those involved in [Satan's] corrupt and sinful plan."[6]

In this chapter we have seen that when Christians die today they do not have to go to Paradise. Paradise is empty, and nowhere in Scripture do we read that it will ever need to be used again. When a Christian dies today he will go immediately to heaven.

---

[6] James, Edgar C., *Teach Yourself the Bible Series: The Epistles of Peter*, Moody Press, p.22

CHAPTER 7

❦

HEAVEN

Ne Plus Ultra.

That is a Latin expression that means "no more beyond." This motto was adopted by the majority of Spaniards in the day of Christopher Columbus because of their belief that the earth was flat and there was no more to be discovered. After the death of Columbus a memorial was erected in Valladolid, Spain, which, among other things, included a lion ripping the word Ne away from the rest of the motto.

The point of the monument is that Columbus, even if accidentally, proved the motto to be wrong; the monument reads *Plus Ultra,* or "More Beyond."

Indeed, many today still cling to the old motto "no more beyond," because they believe that this life is all there is. Followers of Jesus, however, can identify with the Christopher Columbus statue because we truly believe that there is more—much more—beyond.

Heaven—a place that everyone wants to go when they die; a place that everyone wants to know what it looks like; a place that everyone wants to know when they will go there; a place that we use to comfort each other in hard times; and yet, a place that we know so little about.

Is Heaven Real?

There is no way to prove that heaven is real until after we go there. The obvious problem is that the ones that have been there cannot come back and confirms heaven's existence. NASA will not fly into it, and science will not gather information on it. As Christians we believe that heaven is real because the Bible talks about it, but what about the person that does not believe in the Bible?

Some, even those who say they believe that the Bible is the inspired Word of God, believe that heaven is a state of mind or a kind of dream. To this Billy Graham has written, "Jesus did not ascend to a lofty dreamworld following His resurrection, but returned to sit at the right hand of God (Mark 16:19). Abraham didn't cling to the promise of living in a state of mind; he looked forward to 'a city with foundations, who architect and builder is God (Hebrews 11:10).' The Old Testament heroes of faith longed for a literal place—'a better country—a heavenly one…for [God] has prepared a city for them(v.16).' Jesus told His disciples, 'You know the way to the place where I am going (John 14:4)[7].'"

Dr. James Kennedy has provided two convincing proofs for the existence of heaven: people's persecution and Christ's character. According to Kennedy, the early days of Christianity were sparked by a first hand knowledge that Jesus had come back from the dead. That was not legend or religious propaganda; these disciples saw the crucifixion, the mangled body of the Savior, the empty tomb, and the Resurrected Lord. They knew beyond a doubt that Jesus was alive, and they would rather die than deny.

As Kennedy states, "Although many have died for frauds, they didn't know it." People die for other religions, but that is based on their beliefs; these disciples died because they knew the Resurrection was real. If they staged the empty tomb, they would not have endured awful martyrdom for a fraud.

---

[7]   Graham, Billy, *The Heaven Answer Book,* Thomas Nelson Publishers, p.21

The second piece of evidence that heaven is real is Christ's character. Even Jesus' strongest, most hateful critics will concede that He was a good person, an honest teacher, or at least a decent man. If that is the case, what kind of good, honest, or decent teacher would teach about heaven if He made it up? The character of Christ adds credibility to His claims.[8]

In this chapter we will discuss what heaven looks like and when the judgment will be that will send us there, but first we will start with a solemn reminder of how we get there.

As a pastor it is hard to deal with when a family tries to will a recently deceased loved one into heaven. Their father could have been out of church for the last twenty years, drunk every night, and cursed like a sailor, and when we go to minister to the family we hear them all saying, "He's in a better place." Now I realize two things are true here. I am not the judge of who is in heaven or hell, but simply a fruit inspector (John 15:16), and I realize that these people are grieving. But when they cling to the fact that their loved one repeated a prayer in church when he was six and never went back, well, that is confusing to all the unsaved people in the room. "If he got drunk every night, swore, and never went to church, and he still gets to go to heaven, then I am doing just fine without God."

We need to remember that there is only one way to heaven, and that is through Jesus Christ alone (John 14:6). It is a dangerous game when we try to will others there; instead, let us as believers be busy about trying to convert the unsaved while they are still alive all around us.

We all want to know what heaven looks like. I am asked a lot of questions about what life in heaven will be like. People often ask about their favorite pass times: will there be football in heaven? Or they ask about their favorite food: will there be pecan pie in heaven? Can we eat all the chocolate we want and not gain

---

8   Kennedy, James, *Skeptics Answered,* Multnomah, p.143-144

weight there? Will we be able to fly? Can we walk through walls? And those are just the questions from adults!

This curiosity of heaven has led some to sell books by people who have been there and are reporting back. Or at least that is what they claim. Can God take a human to heaven or let him visit in a dream in order to write a book? Of course He can, but that doesn't mean that He has. I know of one person who did beyond a doubt. His name was John, and the Lord gave him a Revelation.

I would caution the reader to be careful about believing the words of man. God gave us what we need to know about heaven and the New Jerusalem in the New Testament. I realize that this book is also the words of man, but it is based on expounding the Word of God.

The problem with these people who claim to have been there is that they are man-centered. These books and testimonies go on and on about immediately seeing Grandma and hugging old Sunday school teachers, but there is a missing element here, and that, quite sadly, is Jesus Christ. Hebrews 9:27 tells us about the moment we will go to heaven, and Grandma and Sunday school teachers are not mentioned here.

A few years ago I got a call at our church office from a publishing company trying to sell a DVD curriculum that corresponds to a popular book about a man that spent ninety minutes in heaven. When I told the lady that I wasn't interested she seemed quite shocked: *"Don't you want to hear about heaven from a man who's been there?"*

And that question is the epitome of our fantastical culture. Everything I know about heaven comes from people who have actually been there. Jesus spoke about it in John 14, the Holy Spirit inspired others to write about it, and John was given a revelation so that he could record parts too. When reading a book about heaven, including this one, be sure that the author's sources are the Bible and others who are expounding on the Bible.

Another question I am often asked is how the judgment correlates with our going to heaven, and here it is: "And as it is appointed unto men once to die, but after this the judgment (Hebrews 9:27)." This verse shows us several important things about life and death. Every living person has an appointment with death, and whether we like it or not, that is an appointment we will keep. Upon death there are "no returns, no reincarnations, no escape; after death the great evaluation ending in judgment." [9]

This verse also shows us that immediately after our death is our judgment. Matthew 7 shows us that Jesus will be the one present at our judgment, which means that no one will walk down the streets of gold until they have first been judged by Jesus. So if I wrote a book that I said God told me to write, and in it I said that I went to heaven (whether I was in a coma, in surgery, asleep, a car wreck—I've heard them all), and my grandmother came running up to see me and we began to walk towards the bright light, is that in keeping with Hebrews 9:27? Absolutely not.

Another truth we learn from this verse is that we each have a personal judgment. Sometimes we might get the idea that there is one massive judgment day where everyone who has ever lived is standing in a winding line waiting for their turn as if they were trying to get on Space Mountain at Disney World. Then St. Peter yells. "Next!" as the next person steps up in line. At the moment I die I will stand before Jesus and He will say one of two things to me.

He will either say, "I never knew you. Depart from me, you worker of iniquity (Matthew 7:23)." Or He will say, "Well done, thou good and faithful servant (Matthew 25:21)." All the Christians will be allowed into heaven following their judgment, and all the ones who rejected Christ will be sent to hell following theirs. There will be another judgment, called the Great White

---

[9]   Evans Jr., Louis H., *The Preacher's Commentary,* Thomas Nelson Publishers, p.168

Throne Judgment, where the people in hell will be judged again, and from there they will be sent to the lake of fire (Revelation 20:11-15). Charles Ryrie reminds us that "physical death claims the body; Hades claims the soul…[both] are cast into the Lake of Fire, since their work is now done."[10]

The judgment for Christians is not a bad thing. Our judgment is referred to as the Bema Seat. The word judgment sounds scary, and many believe that this will be a time of intense judgment for the sake of punishment, but that simply is not consistent with the idea of Jesus taking our punishment for us. This judgment will be for believers only, and after death, there will be nothing to punish the believers for.

I know I'm not the only Christian who has feared this judgment day. Joni Eareckson Tada had a similar misunderstanding of what this judgment would be like. Writing about her erroneous view of the Bema Seat Tada wrote: I saw myself standing under a marquee of a theater. NOW SHOWING, THE UNCENSORED VERSION OF JONI."

She went on to say, "I don't believe He'll roll an uncut, uncensored version of your life. He won't wear the scowl of a rigid and inflexible judge who bangs the gavel and reads aloud your sins for the court record. No, that already happened at another judgment. The judgment at the cross."[11]

When a Christian is welcomed into heaven Jesus will say, "Well done, thou good and faithful servant (Matthew 25:21/ Luke 19:17)." How do we expect Him to go from saying, "Good job" to saying, "Now here is your punishment"? That doesn't make sense.

What we also have to understand is that God chastens His children to make them better, not to get even. When we receive

[10] Ryrie, Charles, *Everyman's Bible Commentary: Revelation,* Moody Publishers, p.135

[11] Tada, Joni Earekson, *Heaven, Your Real Home* p.53

chastening in life God's goal is to make us more like His Son Jesus; after we die and stand in judgment, what would be the point of God's chastening? Any punishment received at the Bema Seat would be of no benefit.

Some people struggle with the idea of God being good and being a Judge at the same time, but we should not think of God's judgment as being a bad thing. In Henry Thiessen's textbook *Lectures in Systematic Theology* he writes that God will judge us, "not in order to submit to an external law, but as the expression of his own character. The individual will have the opportunity to show why he acted as he did and to know the reasons for his sentence. These are fundamental factors in every righteous government."[12]

The word bema is the Greek word that is used to refer to this judgment in Romans 14:10, which says that we will all "stand before the judgment seat (Bema) of Christ. In Paul's day the bema was the platform that a judge would stand on to watch the Olympic games. From the vantage point of the bema, the judge would be able to tell who came in first place, second place, etc. The winner of the event was then called up to receive his prize of a wreath around his neck.

That is the image behind the word that Paul used to describe the judgment for believers. When I was a child I had a teacher tell me that on Judgment Day God was going to give us all a big spanking; that didn't exactly make me look forward to going to heaven, and it didn't really make me want to love God. The truth is, according to Paul, that our judgment will actually be a time of rewarding.

That is not to say that we will be totally off the hook either. Verses like Matthew 25:14-30 demonstrate how believers will have to give an account of how they used their talents (our use of

---

[12] Thiessen, Henry C., *Lectures in Systematic Theology,* William B. Eerdsmans Publishing Company, p.387

the word talent to refer to abilities comes from this parable[13]). We all love the passage where God promises that He will wipe away the tears from our eyes and put an end to crying once and for all, but we need to know when that happens. That is not a promise that is carried out as soon as a person enters heaven, although I don't think there will be anything to cry about for people in heaven right now. But that verse about God wiping away the tears from our eyes in found in Revelation 21:4.

The context of this verse is after the Great White Throne judgment, not after a person enters heaven. That means that there will be crying in heaven by Christians following the judgment of non-believers. Why? Because we will watch as people are sent to the lake of fire for all of eternity. I believe we will stand there and watch our former classmates, coworkers, neighbors, and friends receive their sentence and know that we did little, if anything, to prevent their fate.

This passage is a grave reminder for us today to stop worrying about being annoying, invasive, or holy rollers; when we see people enter the lake of fire, being "too personal" won't seem like a bad idea any more. After a period of sorrow over the fate of unbelievers and our own shortcomings in the Great Commission, *then* God will wipe away every tear from our eyes, and there will be no more crying.

And yet the Bema Seat will still be about our rewards. In light of all of our mistakes God will still choose to honor us like an Olympian stepping up on the platform. The Bema is also mentioned in II Corinthians 5:10, where it says that we will receive either good or bad, depending on how we conducted ourselves. The bad that can come is not punishment, but a reduction of rewards. In John Walvoord's *The Prophecy Knowledge Handbook* he points out that the illustration that Paul is making is "that of a steward, or a trustee, who has responsibility for handling

---

[13]   *Shepherd's Notes: Matthew,* Holman Reference, p.96

the business affairs of another and eventually reporting what he does with it."

He goes on to conclude that "[T]he issue here is not success or amount of success, but rather the question of faithfulness in using properly what God has given to an individual Christian[14]." It appears that this Bema Seat will be a time where Christians will be rewarded for how faithfully they used their spiritual gifts for the Great Commission. But what about those who failed to use their gifts for the glory of God?

The reader might be thinking of that passage where Paul says, "We must all appear before the judgment seat of Christ, that everyone may receive the things done in his body, according to what he has done, whether good or bad (II Corinthians 5:10)." If we will receive according to the bad we have done, won't there be punishment at the judgment?

The word translated as "bad" can also be translated as worthless[15]. Think about the difference between these two uses of the word bad:

> Bad (as in sinful) results in punishment.
> Bad (as in worthless) results in lack of rewards.

It is this author's opinion that the latter is more in keeping with the concept of forgiveness of the redeemed. If instead the former were true then believers would fear meeting Jesus. Furthermore, the former also negates biblical passages such as Romans 8, which promises no condemnation for believers because of the punishment already placed on Jesus; also Ecclesiastes 7:1 says the day of one's death is better than the day of one's birth. If on the day of my death I had to meet an incensed Judge then my birth would certainly trump my death.

---

[14] Walvoord, John F., *The Prophecy Knowledge Handbook,* Victor Books, p.456

[15] Wiersbe, Warren W., *Be Encouraged,* Victor Books, p.61

Remember, the very concepts of propitiation, atonement, and justification contradict the idea of a day of reckoning with God. As a Christian God's wrath has been appeased (propitiation) by the death of Jesus, my sins have been covered (atoned) by the blood of Jesus, and I have become righteous (justified) by the finished work of Jesus. Any punishment for sin today is to make me better (or sanctified) tomorrow; after life there will be no need for that to occur.

However, this section has looked at Paul's words in II Corinthians 5:10, but it is important to see his conclusion in verse 11. "Therefore (or "because of what I just wrote"), knowing the fear of the Lord, we persuade others." In all the excitement of the Bema Seat, one would still be wise to keep the fear of the Lord in mind. Believers must persuade fellow believers to strive to live life the way that God has called us to live it.

The best conclusion this author can come to in light of all the evidence is that The Judgment Seat of Christ will be the ultimate display of truth and grace. As believers who have finished the course and fought a good fight, we will still be humbled by how much more we could have done. In the presence of the one who literally gave all for us, we will understand just how minuscule our efforts were—filthy rags at best. But as this truth comes into focus, so will the amazing grace that we so often sang about on earth, that in light of how self-absorbed even the best of us was, we will still stand before Christ to be rewarded for the comparatively small amount of good that we did.

There are two schools of thought as to when this Bema Seat judgment will take place. One belief is that it will take place after the rapture. In I Thessalonians 4:13-18 Paul wrote to the church at Thessalonica to tell them about the rapture, but there is no mention of the judgment seat taking place there. The other belief is that we will each have a personal judgment seat appearance directly after our death.

In *The Great Doctrines of the Bible* William Evans has written "the erroneous idea that there is to be one great general judgment which is to take place at the end of the world, when all mankind shall stand before the great white throne, is to be guarded against. The judgments of the Bible differ as to time, place, subjects, and results."[16]

The Scriptures never tell us with any certainty, but the latter belief does appear to be more in keeping with Hebrews 9:27's claim that we each have an appointment with death and then the judgment. The only problem is that the word judgment used in Hebrews is different from the word bema used in Romans and I Corinthians.

What is important, then, is not getting caught up in debating exactly when this particular judgment seat will occur. The Bible says it will occur, and it must be after we die, so when it happens is not really important.

Crowns

Throughout the New Testament we see teachings on different crowns that can be received as rewards following the judgment. The five crowns are the incorruptible crown, and the crowns of rejoicing, life, righteousness, and glory.

The incorruptible crown. I Corinthians 9:24-25 says, "Don't you know that they which run in a race run all, but one receives the prize? So run, that you may obtain. And every man that strives for the mastery is temperate in all things. Now they do it to obtain a corruptible crown; but we an incorruptible." This incorruptible crown is given to believers who "run the race" of life in accordance with God's word.

The crown of rejoicing. Some have called this the soul winner's crown, given those who bring others to Christ. I

---

[16]   Evans, William, *The Great Doctrines of the Bible,* Moody Press, p.254

Thessalonians 2:19 says, "For what is our hope, or joy, or crown of rejoicing before our Lord Jesus at his coming? Is it not you?"

The crown of life. This crown is introduced in James 1:12: "Blessed is the man that endures temptation: for when he is tried, he shall receive the crown of life, which the Lord has promised to them that love him." Others call this the martyr's crown, given to the Christians who suffer for the cause of Christ.

The crown of righteousness. At the end of Paul's life he wrote that "there is laid up for me a crown of righteousness, which the Lord, the righteous judge, shall give me at that day: and not to me only, but unto all them also that love his appearing (II Timothy 4:8)." This is a crown given to the believers who eagerly await the return of Christ and live their lives in light of His return.

The crown of glory. This crown is not available to every Christian, but is reserved for those faithful ministers of the gospel. After giving instruction to pastors, I Peter 5:4 says, "And when the chief Shepherd shall appear, you shall receive a crown of glory that fades not away."

This list of crowns has been included to reinforce the idea of the Bema seat being about rewards. It should also be noted that Christians will not wear these crowns for eternity, but they will be given back as an offering to the only one who is worthy of them anyway, and that is King Jesus. Revelation 4:10-11 foretells of believers around the throne casting their crowns at the feet of Jesus.

We have looked at the judgment, and now another thing that is not really all that important is what heaven will look like. I say that because we should not make our decision about whether or not we go to heaven based on the scenery or square footage; at the same time, there is nothing wrong with studying what the Bible says about heaven.

Before we look at what will be in heaven, first we will debunk a myth about heaven. This might come as a shock to the reader, but we will not have our own mansions in heaven. The only time mansions are mentioned in the Bible is in John 14:2 where Jesus says, "In my Father's house are many mansions; if it were not so I would have told you. I go to prepare a place for you."

The word that is used for mansion means "a dwelling or abode." According to the Dictionary, the word mansion means, "a very large, impressive, or stately residence." Obviously there is a discrepancy between these two words. This is not a biblical error, however; this is just an example of how the meanings of words can change over time. The New American Standard Bible, which uses the same texts as the King James Bible, uses "dwelling places" instead of mansions in John 14:2.

So in heaven there are many dwelling places, but that does not mean that we will all have our own small house. Notice that Jesus doesn't say that there are many dwelling places in heaven, but in his Father's house.

Jesus used a different word for His Father's house than he did for the dwelling places. This goes back to an ancient Jewish custom. In those days there would be a house that was owned by the head of the household. When his son was grown and ready to be married, he would begin to prepare a dwelling place for himself and his bride to be; this dwelling place would be an add on to the father's house. So after the young man would propose marriage to his future bride, he would leave her with a promise: I am going to prepare a place for you; be ready, for when I come again I will marry you and we will go to live in my father's house.

For that reason the young bride had to be watchful, for she didn't know when the groom was going to return. She had to be ready for the marriage ceremony at a moment's notice. After the wedding, they would go to live in the dwelling place the groom had prepared in his father's house.

That is exactly what Jesus was saying to the church, the Bride of Christ (Revelation 21:9). We need to be ready at any moment, for the Groom may return for the marriage ceremony.

In the meantime, He has been preparing us dwelling places in His Father's house.

Often we may joke as Christians about who our neighbors will be in heaven. We might say something like, "I hope my mansion is not going to be beside yours!" We act as if we will each have a different address and live on different roads; maybe my mansion will be at the corner of Christ Court and Spirit Street. But the truth is we will all live in the Father's house.

Another myth is that we will all become angels and sit on clouds while we play the harp. The Bible doesn't mention us playing the harp or sitting on clouds, but it does say that we will not become angels. Angels are separate beings from humans, and all of the angels were created before Adam and Eve were. Mathew 22:30 says that people in heaven will not get married, but instead will be "like the angels." It does not say they will be angels, but will be like them; they will be like angles in that they will not get married.

A further proof that we will not become angels in heaven is found in Hebrews 12:22-23. This verse shows that people in New Jerusalem will be met both by angels and by the spirits of just men made perfect. This verse makes a clear distinction between angels and those believers who have died and been made perfect. "Humans never become angels, and angels never become human."[17]

A third and final myth about heaven is that after we get there we will be looking down on everyone on earth. "Don't worry son, Granny is looking down on us today." Do we really think people in heaven can look down and watch us on earth? Do we really *want* people in heaven to look down and watch us on earth?

Think about it. Without trying to be crude, do you really want your loved ones who have passed on to be able to see you?

[17]   Southard, Randy, *The World's Easiest Guide for New Believers,* Northfield Press, p.155

What if they decide to take a peek at us when we are in the shower? That wouldn't be fun for anybody. I also don't believe they would want to look down at a sinful world, especially when they have the ability to spend time with Jesus.

Now let's shift gears and look at some things we do know will be in heaven. First of all, and most importantly, God will be in heaven. In Psalm 103:19 we see that God has established His throne in heaven. Like a palace in the royal court, so God has a throne room in heaven from which He rules His creation.

Why would His throne be in heaven and not on earth? Charles Spurgeon, that great "Prince of Preachers," has pointed out that "his dominion is not disputed there by the angels that attend him, as it is on earth by the rebels that arm themselves again him... The heavens are the loftiest part of the creation, and the only fit palace for him."[18]

There are many verses that refer to God as being in heaven, but consider just this one: when Jesus was asked by the disciples to teach them how to pray, He began His model prayer by saying, "Our Father who art in heaven (Matthew 6:9)."

Since the Bible also teaches the concept of the Trinity, that God, Jesus, and the Spirit are one, then we know that the Son and the Spirit are also in heaven. Jesus admitted that He came down from heaven in John 6:38, and when the Holy Spirit came down on the Day of Pentecost in Acts 2:2, He was accompanied by a sound from heaven like a mighty, rushing wind. The martyr Stephen served as a witness to the fact that Jesus returned to heaven, for at his execution, "God granted him a vision of the glorified Jesus"[19] as he saw "Jesus standing on the right hand of God (Acts 7:55)."

---

[18] Spurgeon, Charles, *The Treasury of David,* Hendrickson Publishers, p.295-296

[19] Kent Jr., Homer A., *Jerusalem to Rome: Studies in Acts,* Baker Book House, p.71

We also know that angels are there. We recently saw that there are angels that are separate from humans, and that they dwell in heaven. When John was on Patmos he received a revelation from the Lord, and he got a glimpse of the throne room of God in heaven. In Revelation 5:11 John writes about the angels around the throne who are crying out with a loud voice, "Worthy is the Lamb that was slain, to receive power, and riches, and wisdom, and strength, and honor, and glory, and blessing."

There is one other thing about heaven that is there, and that is our citizenship if we have been born again (Philippians 3:10). Other than that, we don't know much about what heaven will look like. You might be thinking, *What about the streets of gold? What about the pearly gates?*

Those details are recorded as being part of another heaven.

A new heaven.

CHAPTER 8

NEW JERUSALEM

In previous chapters we have seen that hell is not eternal, but that the lake of fire is. In the same way, the heaven that people are in now is not eternal either. In Revelation 21:1 John recorded that he saw a "new heaven and a new earth, for the first heaven and the first earth were passed away."

This earth that we are currently living on will pass away and be replaced by a new earth. The context of Revelation 21 is after everything—the rapture, the Great Tribulation, and life on earth in general. That passage does not say that this earth passed away because mankind was a poor steward of this planet, or that it passed away due to aerosol cans; this planet will make it to the end and then it will be destroyed and replaced.

But in addition to this earth passing away and being replaced, so the current heaven will also be replaced. The Bible doesn't say much about this new heaven, but it doesn't really matter because we will not be living in it. The next verse in the chapter tells us about a new city that we will live in on earth.

"And I, John, saw the holy city, new Jerusalem, coming down from God out of heaven." This new city will be where all believers will live with God. The Great White Throne Judgment will not have taken place yet, so all unbelievers will be in hell, and none will be on the earth.

Verse three continues, "And I heard a great voice out of heaven saying, 'Behold, the tabernacle of God is with men, and He shall dwell with them, and they shall be His people, and God Himself shall be with them, and be their God." Now we have God coming to dwell on earth with men, the way He originally intended to. This is similar to how God would walk with Adam in the Garden of Eden in the cool of the day (Genesis 3:8), and once there is no more sin, God will be able to live among us.

After that verse we begin to get a little description of what New Jerusalem will look like. Beginning in verse 11 we see that New Jerusalem will have crystal clear light, and that it is a walled city. There are twelve gates within the walls, and an angel sits on each gate. The repetition of the number twelve is symbolic of the twelve tribes of Israel. There will also be twelve foundation stones, and this number twelve represents the twelve apostles.

This author believes that the Bible should be understood literally, but that it is also rich in symbolism. For example, when 21st Century Americans read about the walls of this city we don't typically think about them the same way that 1st Century Jews did. In our world of missile defense and military might we don't associate walls with protection, but the original audience of the New Testament would hear about these walls and think of safety.

It is possible that New Jerusalem will actually have these high walls, but it is also possible that John was just trying to paint a picture of total safety for all of the city's inhabitants. Either way, the point is that God will be in charge and there will be nothing that can bring us harm.

The dimensions of that great city are staggering. The city will be a perfect square, having all of its sides the same length, and each of those sides is 1,500 (12,000 furlongs) miles long. It might be hard to grasp what those measurements look like, but as a native Floridian I used make the drive from Orlando, Florida to Dallas, Texas when I was a college student in the Dallas/Fort Worth area. That drive was roughly 1,300 miles each way, which means that driving straight through, which took around 18 hours, would not even compare to the length of one of the four walls of New Jerusalem.

Bible scholar Henry Morris postulated that with these dimensions there would be 75 acres for every one person. (He estimated there will have been 100 billion people to live on earth, and that 20% would be saved. Obviously there is no way to get an actual number of residents of this city until we get there, but that is still an interesting figure.)

If it is still hard to wrap your mind around all of this, a perfect square with 1,500-mile sides is almost the exact size of our moon.

It is also interesting to note that the measurement of each side of the new city correlates with the diameter of the earth. The earth's diameter is 7,920 miles long, while each side of New Jerusalem is 7,920,000 feet long. Many years before anyone would be able to calculate the diameter of our planet, the Creator gave John the dimensions of a city that won't be around for many years still, and the digits of the two are very similar.

John then proceeds to give us a list of all the precious stones that are used as building blocks for the city walls and foundations, and then we read that New Jerusalem, not heaven, has streets of gold. This is not to say that there are no streets of gold in heaven today, but the only biblical reference to streets of gold is referring to New Jerusalem.

Just like with the potential symbolism of the city's high walls, the same case can be made for these precious stones that are listed. It is interesting that the diamond is not listed among them, but today we know just how valuable diamonds are (and that they are a girl's best friend). John's original audience would not be impressed to hear about diamonds there because they were so difficult to mine that they were considered worthless. At the time he wrote this pearls were considered to be the most precious stone, and John highlights them. So once again, this might not mean that it is pearls and no diamonds, or diamonds and no pearls;

the point could well be that this city is rich in beauty and wealth, far beyond anything we can comprehend.

The rest of chapter 21 reveals things that will not be in the new city. There will not be a tabernacle or church building because the Lord God Almighty and the Lamb are the temple. There will not be a sun or moon because Jesus is the light of the city. There will be no night, so the gates will never be closed. Of course, invasions typically would take place under the cover of darkness, but in this city there will be no invasions, so the gates would never need to be closed anyway.

John also records that there will be no sea (21:1). This might be figurative, for in John's day the sea was dangerous and ever changing, and it was also the place where the Beast of Revelation 13 would come from. But the reference to no sea could also be literal. It's not like we will need a sea anyway.

Verse 4 lists several other things that will not be in this holy city: "there shall be no more death, neither sorrow, nor crying, neither shall there be any more pain." What an amazing thought! It is hard to even conceive of such a place, for in this world we are all too acquainted with that cruel quartet of death, sorrow, crying, and pain.

The reason those things will no longer be around is explained at the end of the verse: "for the former things have passed away." The former things include the curse and the subsequent punishment. People always ask why bad things happen to good people, and the theological answer is that we live on a cursed planet. Once Adam and Eve took a foolish bite of that forbidden fruit God cursed the ground they walked on, and now "death has passed upon all men, for that all have sinned (Romans 5:12)."

One final listing of things that will not be on the new earth is found in the final verse of the chapter, verse 27. It says that nothing will enter into the city that will defile it, neither those who practice abominations or tell lies. Sin and Satan will have been defeated once and for all, and nothing will creep into the city to defile it.

A distinction between the New Earth and New Jerusalem

In Revelation 21 it begins by describing the New Earth in the first eight verses. But in verses 9-10 John writes that angels came and took him to a high mountain to show him another city, and there he begins his description of New Jerusalem.

These should not be though of as separate places, just as Earth and Jerusalem are not separate places today. Earth is a planet, and Jerusalem is one city on this planet. In the same way, New Jerusalem will be a city on the New Earth.

On this current Earth Jerusalem is the city that God has sovereignly chosen to be His holy city, so it only makes sense that on the New Earth New Jerusalem will be His holy city still. That is why John records that the presence of God is in this new holy city (21:11, 22-23).

CHAPTER 9

❦

THE GARDEN OF EDEN

The Garden of Eden is described in Genesis 2:8-17. Most people are quite familiar with this garden, for it was the birthplace of sin on earth. The snake, the fruit, the bite—even Adam and Eve's seemingly odd nudity are all childhood Bible stories.

You might even be wondering why we are shifting from the end of the story back to the beginning. How does one turn from Revelation 21 back to Genesis 2? It is really amazing how Genesis 1-2 tie in with Revelation 22.

First, let's look at the details recorded about the Garden. The first thing we see is that the Garden was created for man's benefit. Before any other details are listed, Genesis 2:8 says that "God planted a garden...and there He put the man that He had formed." We know that "man" is Adam.

Next we see what the Lord planted in this garden. "Every tree that is pleasant to the sight, and good for food; the tree of life... and the tree of knowledge of good and evil."

After that we see that God put a river in the garden to keep it watered (it never rained prior to the Great Flood), and then the Bible mentions different natural minerals, such as gold, dbellium, and onyx stones. The body of water that kept Eden hydrated must have been quite large because it split into four different rivers. The rivers are listed by name, and we recognize the Tigris (Hiddekel) and Euphrates Rivers, but the other two, Gihon and Pishon, are not known today. Henry Morris postulated that those rivers most likely lost their identity after the Flood[20].

Then there are the famous trees. There is the tree of life (verse 9) and the tree of knowledge of good and evil (verse 17). The tree of life was placed in the center of the garden, and most believe that by eating from its fruit Adam and Eve would have lived forever. Instead, they chose to eat the forbidden fruit from the tree of knowledge of good and evil.

The name of this second tree suggests that evil was already present in the world, even though Adam had not yet sinned; evil was present, but they had no knowledge of it. But in order for Satan to be the tempter of Genesis 3 he would already have sinned and rebelled from heaven, so that is how evil could already be present. Nevertheless, God told Adam that he would surely die if he ate from that tree.

God also gave Adam dominion over the garden. He was charged to work the field, and he could eat whatever he wanted. Some people think that work came as a result of the fall, but Adam was already told to work. After the fall God told Adam that he would work "from the sweat of his brow." Work changed after the fall, but good, wholesome work is a God-ordained part of life, and God Himself modeled that for us during the Creation, when on the seventh day "God rested on the seventh day from all His work (Genesis 2:2)."

"Work isn't a curse;" wrote Warren Wiersbe. "It's an opportunity to use our abilities and opportunities in cooperating with God and being faithful stewards of His creation[21]."

As we know, Satan tempted Eve to eat the fruit of the tree of knowledge of good and evil, and she took a bite. She then gave Adam some fruit, and he ate it too. Once they did God cursed the

---

[20]   Morris, Henry M., *The Genesis Record,* Baker Book House, p.89

[21]   Wiersbe, Warren W., *Be Basic,* David C. Cook, p.39

ground, causing thorns to grow, sweat to drip, pain in childbirth, and ultimately eviction from the Garden of Eden (Genesis 3:24). Never again would mankind dwell in a sinless paradise on Earth.

God kicked Adam and Eve out of the Garden, and He placed two Cherubim at the gate to stand guard. Evangelist Rick Coram described these creatures as "angelic guards" that kept them from the Garden.[22]

A New Garden of Eden

The Bible begins with God creating the heavens and the earth, but then man sinned and the planet was cursed. The rest of the Bible is the result of Adam's choice to sin. Sacrifices were needed, then a Savior came to be sacrificed, and now we are waiting for the Lord's return. After the Great Tribulation God will destroy this planet, and then the Bible ends just like it began: God creates heaven and earth.

The Bible's final chapter mentions some of the same elements that were created in the opening chapter. We see a glassy river, which is the crystal sea that many people associate with heaven, which proceeds from God's throne. Then we read about the tree of life again, which will produce a different fruit for each month of the year.

In the original Garden of Eden this tree of life would have provided Adam and Eve immortality, but in the New Jerusalem we read that it exists for the "healing of the nations." The biggest difference between the original Garden and this Eden-like state is the promise of Revelation 22:3, which prophesies that "there will be no more curse."

With this promise the Bible has come full circle. God's original plan was to create Earth to be an Edenic paradise, and when it is all said and done, it will be. So heaven as it exists

---

[22]   Coram, Rick, *Surrounded by Angels,* Evangel Publications, p.116

today is not our eternal home, but heaven on earth in the New Jerusalem will last for all eternity.

So where is the Garden of Eden now? It was present in the Middle East shortly after Creation, and it will be in the New Jerusalem after the Tribulation, but where is it today? We certainly cannot say with 100% certainty, but many believe that God drew the Garden up to heaven where it waits until He is ready to plant it back on earth again.

CHAPTER 10

❦

GAHENNA

Since this book has addressed Hades, hell, and the lake of fire, among other things, it seems only fitting to explore Gahenna as well. Gahenna is the word that is translated as hell in the New Testament twelve times.

It is almost funny how some people teach that Jesus did not believe in a literal hell, and yet out of the twelve uses of Gahenna, Jesus used the word eleven times. The only other reference came from the epistle of James, the half-brother of Jesus.

Some now teach that Jesus was not referring to a literal place where souls will actually be tormented in flames. Some have tried to paint Gahenna as simply the town garbage dump. Perhaps, like me, you have been told that Gahenna was where the Jews' trash was taken to be burned.

In Rob Bell's controversial book *Love Wins,* he describes Gahenna this way:

> "People tossed their garbage and waste into this valley. There was a fire there, burning constantly to consume the trash. Wild animals fought over the scraps of food along the edges of the heap. When they fought their teeth would make a gnashing sound. Gahenna was the place with the gnashing of teeth, where the fire never went out.

Gahenna was an actual place that Jesus' listeners would
have been familiar with. So the next time someone asks
you if you believe in an actual hell, you can always say,
'Yes, I do believe that my garbage goes somewhere...'"[23]

The mention of gnashing of teeth is a reference to the New
Testament descriptions of Gahenna. One such reference is Luke
13:28, which says: There shall be weeping and gnashing of teeth,
when ye shall see Abraham, and Isaac, and Jacob, and all the
prophets, in the kingdom of God, and you yourselves thrust out.

It is interesting that Mr. Bell didn't have an answer for the
weeping part, simply the gnashing of teeth. Perhaps the wild
animals that did not get any scraps were weeping. And what does
he do with the second half of the verse? Abraham, Isaac, Jacob,
and the prophets, all in the kingdom of God, as the unsaved
person is "thrust out" of the kingdom.

Not thrust out of the garbage dump.

It is obvious that Jesus is referring to a place of real punishment
when He taught about Gahenna. But was Gahenna an actual
garbage dump that Jesus used as a word picture?

There is no evidence whatsoever to support the claim that
Gahenna was a garbage dump when Jesus alluded to it. It is not
up to me to prove that it wasn't one; it is up to the person who
claims that it was to prove it.

The first person to ever claim that Gahenna was a dump was
in the year 1200, over a thousand years after Jesus' resurrection.
The man who said it, Rabbi David Kimhi, was a European, not
an Israelite. And in his letter he says that the fact that Gahenna had
become a garbage dump was a fitting analogy of the judgment.

Just for the sake of argument, consider that Gahenna actually
was simply the town dump when Jesus was on earth. Like Kimhi
said, that only serves as an object lesson to what hell is. As Francis

---

[23]   Bell, Rob, *Love Wins,* Harper Collins, p.68

Chan so wisely points out in his book *Erasing Hell* (which was a rebuttal of *Love Wins)*, sometimes we refer to the freeway as a parking lot when traffic is backed up, but nobody thinks it is a *real* parking lot. No one would stop on the freeway, turn off the car, and go about their business for the day.

The fact that a parking lot is a real place allows the person to grasp the picture of the backed up freeway, and the fact that Gahenna is a real place allowed Jesus' listeners to grasp His point.[24]

So if Gahenna was not a garbage dump, then what was it? We can actually go back to the Old Testament to find out. There are a handful of references to the Valley of the son of Hinnom (or *Gahenna)* in the Old Testament.

In a moment we will look at the verses that give us a description as to what took place in this valley, but first notice that those verses are bookended by geographical references. Joshua 15:8 and 18:16 both list this valley as marking a border in the Promised Land. Then Nehemiah 11:30 mentions the valley as a place that was inhabited after the Babylonian captivity.

We see from these verses that Gahenna, or the Valley of the Son of Hinnom, or even the Valley of Hinnom, was an actual place. Now look at what these next verses tell us about what happened in that valley.

II Chronicles 28:3 tells us that the evil King Ahaz "burnt incense in the valley of the son of Hinnom, and burnt his children in the fire, after the abominations of the heathen whom the LORD had cast out before the children of Israel."

This man sacrificed his own children in the Valley of Hinnom, and observe his method of sacrificing them: he burnt them in the fire. Not all of Ahaz's children were sacrificed though; we know that later his son succeeded him on the throne, so he at least kept a son alive for the sake of an heir. But his son's son, Manasseh, continued the same practice as his grandfather Ahaz:

---

[24]   Chan, Francis, *Erasing Hell,* David C. Cook, p.59

> And [Manasseh] caused his children to pass through
> the fire in the valley of the son of Hinnom: also he
> observed times, and used enchantments, and used
> witchcraft, and dealt with a familiar spirit, and with
> wizards: he wrought much evil in the sight of the
> LORD, to provoke him to anger (II Chronicles 33:6).

It was in this valley pagans sacrificed their children to the gods
Molech and Baal. Consider these other verses: Isaiah 30:33, 66:24
(compared to Mark 9:44-48), II Kings 16:3, 21:6, and 23:10, and
Ezekiel 16:20-21.

The prophet Jeremiah wrote that eventually the valley would
no longer be called Gahenna but the Valley of Slaughter (Jeremiah
7:31-32). By the time Jesus was walking on earth His Jewish
audience would have been well aware of this prophecy, and they
would fully understand that He was using this valley with its
horrible history as a word picture for the most horrible place in
the universe.

So how should we best understand Gahenna today? Gahenna
should be thought of as synonymous with the lake of fire. When
Jesus taught about hell as the place that those who have died
without Christ go, He used the word Hades, which we have seen
is only a holding cell. When He spoke of everlasting punishment,
He used Gahenna.

One day hell will be cast into Gahenna, or the lake of fire.
The problem with the garbage dump analogy is that garbage is
eventually consumed and then ceases to exist, but that will not
happen to the unbelievers in the lake of fire, for Jesus said it will
be a place of "everlasting punishment (Matthew 25:46)."

Jesus did not go to Gahenna after His death because no one is
yet in Gahenna. Death and hell, along with its tenants, will one
day be cast there, but there was no reason for Jesus to have gone
to Gahenna.

CHAPTER 11

❦

TARTARUS

There is one final word on hell that must be discussed in order to make this book complete. Peter used a word that has been translated as hell in II Peter 2:4, and that Greek word is Tartarus. Here is the verse:

> "For if God spared not the angels that sinned, but cast them down to hell, and delivered them into chains of darkness, to be reserved unto judgment…"

Peter's thought is continued in verses 5-6. He gives examples of how God did not spare the world, but destroyed humanity, minus Noah's family, and He likewise later destroyed the inhabitants of Sodom and Gomorrah, minus Lot's family. If God did not spare them, then why would He spare the ungodly that Peter is referring to? This is another sermon for another day, but a good sermon nonetheless.

What is this Tartarus that Peter speaks of, and why are there angels chained up there? Those questions will be discussed in this chapter.

One of the problems with Tartarus is that it appears to be present in mythology prior to the New Testament. This has led critics of the Bible to say that the gospel writers simply borrowed from the ancient mythology.

For example, in 380 BC Plato wrote in *Georgias* that souls are judged after death, and those deserving of punishment were sentenced to Tartarus. Elsewhere in mythology Tartarus was seen as a pit where the damned were sent, or as an abyss ruled by the Titan gods, making it a place even worse than Hades. Essentially, Tartarus was viewed as being a place reserved for the worst of the worst.

Peter clearly borrowed this word from mythology, but that does not mean that the concept of hell is a myth. What is more likely is that the Greek writers like Plato borrowed the concept from the Old Testament teachings on sheol (which is translated as hades in Greek). For centuries prior to Greek mythology the Scriptures taught that the unregenerate would have their fate sealed in the heart of the earth, so technically the Greeks built a legend out of Biblical teaching.

Peter, then, was not teaching a myth; he was simply using a concept, like Gahenna, that his listeners would understand. This is no different than Jesus using farming or fishing analogies for his farmer and fishermen audiences.

But Peter could have chosen to use the word Gahenna or hades, so why did he use Tartarus? Was he trying to make a distinction?

Peter is the first to mention angels being in hell. These should not be thought of as the angels of heaven, but rather as demons, or fallen angels. Remember, Satan was once an angel named Lucifer, and he chose to rebel against God (Isaiah 14:12-15, Ezekiel 28:11-19). Once Lucifer's pride got the better of him and he rebelled, he was evicted from heaven. Listen to how John Milton described how Lucifer must have later felt:

> "O sun, to tell thee how I hate thy beams that bring to
> my remembrance from what state I fell, how glorious

once above thy sphere, till pride and worse ambition
threw me down, warring in Heaven against Heaven's
Matchless King!"[25]

But Satan did not leave alone. In Revelation 12:4 we get the
idea that a third of the angels of heaven chose to join Lucifer in
his revolt, and they too were cast down from heaven. Today Satan
walks around the earth "as a roaring lion, seeking whom he may
devour (I Peter 5:8)," and that believers are at war against demons
(Ephesians 6:12).

But this verse from II Peter says that some are chained up
waiting for the judgment. Bible scholar Warren Wiersbe concludes
"Tartarus may be a special section of hell where these angels are
chained in pits of darkness, awaiting the final judgment."[26] Jude
6 also mentions these demons:

"And the angels which kept not their first estate,
but left their own habitation, he hath reserved in
everlasting chains under darkness unto the judgment
of the great day."

The angels that are chained up in Tartarus, according to Jude,
are the ones that left their natural habitations. This appears to be
a reference back to Genesis 6, just before the Great Flood. In that
chapter the Bible teaches that some of the fallen angels ("sons
of God") actually procreated with human women (this most
likely happened through possessing human males). This was so
detestable to God that apparently He had them chained up in hell,
where they will be until they are thrown into the Lake of Fire.

Writing about this verse in his widely used study Bible, John
MacArthur writes, "The Jews eventually came to use [Tartarus]

25   Milton, John, *Paradise Lost,* taken from *The Norton Anthology of World
      Masterpieces,* 7th edition, volume 1, W.W. Norton & Company, p.2199
26   Wiersbe, Warren W., *Be Alert,* Victor Books, p.42

to describe the place where fallen angles were sent. It defined for them the lowest hell, the deepest pit, the most terrible place of torture and eternal suffering."[27]

Peter, then, used Tartarus to illustrate a place for the worst of the worst. This is where some beings, which were once perfect angels, rebelled against God and followed Lucifer, then had immoral relations with women.

Jesus, then, did not spend any time in Tartarus. This place is only mentioned once in Scripture, and there is nothing there that would indicate that Jesus went, or even needed to go to Tartarus to redeem mankind.

---

[27] MacArthur, John, *The MacArthur Study Bible,* Crossway, notes on II Peter 2:4, p.1905

CHAPTER 12

❧

PURGATORY

What about purgatory? Could purgatory have been an option for Jesus? He certainly didn't have to be in the flames of Hades, and He said that He didn't go to heaven, so maybe He went to more of a neutral place in purgatory.

While that might sound like a good idea we must conclude that it is not true. In order for Jesus to have gone to purgatory, purgatory would have to be an actual place.

What is purgatory?

Purgatory is taught to be a place in between earth and heaven. According to the Catholic website newadvent.org, purgatory is "a place or condition of temporal punishment for those who, departing this life in God's grace, are not entirely free from venial faults, or have not fully paid the satisfaction due to their transgressions."

The word purgatory comes from the Latin word *purgatorium,* and it means, "to make clean or purify." Contrary to popular opinion, purgatory is not a place where the unsaved have a chance to be regenerated; it is only a place where those about to enter heaven still have some punishment to go through.

In the 14th Century Dante published his famed *Divine Comedy,* which was a trilogy consisting of *Inferno, Purgatorio,* and *Paradisio.*

The allegory charts a journey from hell (inferno), through purgatory, and eventually into heaven. In purgatory, according to Dante, one must ascend the seven levels of suffering and growth (associated with the seven deadly sins).

Purgatorio opens this way: "To course across more kindly waters now my talent's little vessel lifts her sails, leaving behind herself a sea so cruel; and what I sing will be that second kingdom, in which the human soul is cleansed from sin, becoming worthy of ascent to heaven."[28]

One can't help but wonder where the idea of such a place originated. The word purgatory is not found in the Bible, and while that does not disqualify its validity, it is still a good place to begin.

The Bible teaches that God exists in a Trinity, that Jesus is coming to rapture the church, and that there is an age of accountability where each person becomes responsible for choosing to follow Christ. But as stated in the third chapter, the words trinity, rapture, and "age of accountability" do not appear in the Bible. Those concepts do not become void, though, because there is strong Scriptural support for each of those three instances.

The fact that the word purgatory is not found in the Bible does not immediately rule it out, but the only way we can continue to entertain the idea is if there is Scriptural support for it. Proponents of purgatory use two references to support their claim: I Corinthians 3:10-15 and II Maccabees 12:42-46. Here is the passage from I Corinthians:

> *"According to the grace of God which is given unto me, as a wise master builder, I have laid the foundation, and another buildeth thereon. But let every man take heed how he buildeth thereupon. For other foundation can no man lay than that is laid, which is Jesus Christ. Now if any man*

---

[28] Alighieri, Dante, *Purgatorio*, taken from *The Norton Anthology of World Masterpieces*, 7th edition, volume 1, W.W. Norton & Company, p.1409

> *build upon this foundation gold, silver, precious stones, wood,*
> *hay, stubble; every man's work shall be made manifest: for*
> *the day shall declare it, because it shall be revealed by fire;*
> *and the fire shall try every man's work of what sort it is. If*
> *any man's work abide which he hath built thereupon, he shall*
> *receive a reward. If any man's work shall be burned, he shall*
> *suffer loss: but he himself shall be saved; yet so as by fire."*

This passage speaks of things being burned in the fire, but it should not be thought of as purgatory. This passage is in keeping with the teachings of Jesus and the apostles that, at the end of each person's life, everything will be stripped away, and only what was important will really last.

Jesus taught about separating the wheat from the tares and burning the chaff—all farming terms—to portray the judgment of Christians. In the end, the only things that will matter are whether a person believed in Jesus Christ, and if he lived his life for the Lord.

This is also in keeping with the Bema Seat, which was discussed in the chapter on heaven. On that day we will be rewarded as Olympians. Notice the reference to rewards in the I Corinthians passage.

So this section of Scripture doesn't seem to be teaching a new idea of purgatory, but instead is continuing the theme of rewards after this life. Now let's examine the passage from II Maccabees:

> *"And they begged him that this sin might be completely*
> *blotted out. Then, Judas, that great man, urged the people*
> *to keep away from sin, because they had seen for themselves*
> *what had happened to those men who had sinned. He also*
> *took up a collection from all his men, totaling about four*
> *pounds of silver, and sent it to Jerusalem to provide for a sin*
> *offering. Judas did this noble thing because he believed in*
> *the resurrection of the dead. If he had not believed that the*
> *dead would be raised, it would have been foolish and useless*

> to pray for them. In his firm and devout conviction that all
> of God's faithful people would receive a wonderful reward,
> Judas made provision for a sin offering to set free from their
> sin those who had died."

In this passage the Jews had just finished fighting a battle, and the bodies of the fallen soldiers were being collected for burial. It was discovered that each of the deceased men had a similar necklace with an inscription of an idol on it, and everyone realized that these men had died in battle because of their sin of idolatry.

That is what prompted Judas to take up an offering and pray for these idolatrous men. The passage states that he believed in the resurrection of the dead, so this act was done on behalf of the dead soldiers.

There are several problems with these verses. The second problem will be discussed later under the topic of mortal vs. venial sins, and the first problem is this: II Maccabees (or I Maccabees for that matter) is not a part of the original Bible.

When the Bible originally came together each book had to meet the canon. That means that every book in today's Bible was found to have been inspired (literally "breathed") by God and historically accurate. The word canon simply means "measuring stick," and the canon is said to be a "closed canon," meaning that no future books can be added.

There are Gnostic gospels, such as the Gospel of Thomas, for example, that did not meet the canon. This book was decided to not have been inspired due to the nature of the content (for example, Jesus is recorded there as saying, "Blessed is every female that makes herself male."). There are also Apocryphal books, such as I and II Maccabees, that are part of the Catholic Bible.

Books in the Apocrypha are considered by the Catholics to be "deuterocanonical," which means "belonging to the second canon." The obvious problem here is that after the canon, the canon was closed so that there could not be a second canon. Who is to say no if someone wants a third canon? The canon was closed to prevent heretical books from creeping into the Bible.

When Jesus was on earth in the New Testament He routinely was in the synagogue on the Sabbath, and on occasions it is even recorded that He did the teaching (who better to teach than the Author?). When Jesus had the scrolls teaching from the Old Testament, which was all they had back then, He never commented that Maccabees was missing from the collection. If God wanted those letters to have been included in His Word, then He would have made sure it was included.

So the word purgatory doesn't appear in the Bible, or even in the Apocrypha, and the only two passages that its defenders turn to for support do not really support it. Why should we believe in a place that is not biblical?

What sends a person to purgatory?

According to it's teaching, people go to purgatory when they have sins that they have not been punished for yet. The traditional Christian teaching is that Christians go to heaven while those who refused Christ choose hell, but those who believe in purgatory believe that there are Christians that have to be punished for sin postmortem.

Paul directly contradicted that idea when he wrote that "there is now no condemnation for those who are in Christ Jesus (Romans 8:1)." How can someone who is in Christ Jesus be condemned to suffer in purgatory?

Catholics, who are the primary champions of purgatory, teach that there are two types of sins, mortal and venial. According to the Vatican's website, mortal sins, they teach, are "grave violations of God's law." They believe that these mortal sins are ones that "turn men away from God."

On the other hand there are venial sins, which are defined as "forgivable sins" that "do not set men in direct opposition to the will and friendship of God." But like the idea of purgatory itself, mortal vs. venial sins are not biblical.

Who decides which sin is a mortal sin, or if one is simply venial? Since the Bible doesn't say, then we are leaving this extra biblical invention to be determined by man. What the Bible does say about sin is "whosoever shall keep the whole law, and yet offend in one point, he is guilty of all (James 2:10)."

So according to the Bible God makes no distinction between sins that directly turn men away from Him and those that do not. James teaches that a person can live his entire life and never commit murder, but if he gossips one time, he is still guilty of murder. The reality is that our sin nature separates us from God, for when Adam and Eve first sinned in the Garden of Eden they passed their sinfulness on to the rest of humanity.

Romans 5:12 says that it was "by one man sin entered into the world, and death by sin, and death passed upon all men for that all have sinned." This verse does not say that some sins are mortal, but that all sins bring death; of course, Revelation 20:14 says that the second death is the lake of fire, which is the ultimate death that Romans 5:12 speaks of.

Just for the sake of argument, consider for a moment that there is a distinction between mortal and venial sins. In Luke 16 Jesus tells the story about a man that died and went to hell, and that man is contrasted with Lazarus, who went to Paradise. In this account there is no mention that the unnamed rich man had committed any gross mortal sins, just that he was stingy with his money and failed to show love to the poor Lazarus.

If this rich man went to hell as the result of committing mortal sins, would that not have been a great teaching moment for Jesus? He could have used that story to tell His disciples, and all subsequent followers, that it was his mortal sins that doomed him to hell; it is also interesting to note that Lazarus did not have to spend any time in purgatory. He was immediately ushered into Abraham's bosom, so the reader is left to assume that either

Lazarus had no venial sins for which he had not been punished, or else purgatory does not exist. Either way, Jesus never mentioned purgatory in His clearest teaching on the afterlife.

Now go back to the passage in II Maccabees 12, where the idolatrous soldiers were slain in battle. In that passage Judas made it clear that everyone understood why these men had died: they had turned from the Lord and were serving idols. If mortal sins, by definition, are sins that turn men away from God, then would this not be a clear mortal sin? How can one possibly turn away from God more than through idolatry?

And yet Judas and his men pray for their comrades and even take up a collection and offer sacrifices on their behalf. This passage is used to support the theory of purgatory, and yet it easily refutes it.

If these men had only committed venial sins, then one could argue that Judas would pray for them in purgatory. But these men committed mortal sins ("grave violations of God's law"), so they should have been in hell with no chance of being resurrected to heaven.

What happens in purgatory?

People in purgatory are not comforted like those in Paradise. The accepted idea is that purgatory is a place of punishment similar to the lake of fire, just not eternal. This idea was birthed from the I Corinthians 3 passage about the dross being burned in the fire. Pope Gregory I wrote that there must exist some purifying fire to cleanse the soul from "minor faults" that had not been purged away.

While a person is being punished for his venial sins in purgatory, his loved ones can pray and offer indulgences to have his "sentence" reduced. This is also littered with poor theology.

For starters, praying for the dead is not biblical (except for the deuterocanonical II Maccabees), and the recipient of those prayers is not either. When praying for a person in purgatory the

Catholics pray to Mary, the mother of Jesus Christ. She is said to be the intercessor for salvation, which is clearly refuted by Scripture, specifically I Timothy 2:5. This verse says that there is "one mediator between God and man, the man Christ Jesus."

This new role for Mary as mediator was taken from a prayer by Saint Ephrem the Syrian, who referred to Mary as "the mediatrix of the whole world." Once again new theology is bred by non-biblical sources.

Another part of the problem with praying for those in purgatory is the idea of indulgences on their behalf. This takes the responsibility off of the offender and allows someone else to "be righteous" on their behalf. Ezekiel 18:20 says, "The soul that sins, it shall die. The son shall not bear the iniquity of the father, neither shall the father bear the iniquity of the son: the righteousness of the righteous shall be upon him, and the wickedness of the wicked shall be upon him."

My relationship with God is purely between He and I; no one else can strengthen our relationship for me. If I choose to live in sin then I must pay the consequences, and no one human, or even Mary, can remove those sins for me.

Another problem lies in the indulgences. Indulgences are basically a way of having one's sins forgiven. There is a belief that a person can make a deposit into a so-called Treasury of Merit, and that by offering indulgences, a person can make investments into this account and receive rewards from God. The Bible clearly teaches that God rewards the faithful (consider Hebrews 11:6, for example), but He does not do this through religious rituals. To offer indulgences one might say a certain number of memorized prayers, give money, or light candles.

Jesus warned against chanting memorized prayers in Matthew 6:7. In II Corinthians 9:7 Paul wrote that each person should give from his heart, not begrudgingly or of necessity, and that the Lord loves a cheerful giver. Therefore, if a person is giving money to the church because he feels like he has to, or if he is giving in order to manipulate some good fortune for himself or another person, then he is not really giving from his heart.

With that in mind consider this next statement. In 2005 the *Compendium of the Catechism of the Catholic Church* was published, which was a summary of the Catechism of the Catholic Church, or the CCC. The CCC is the official teaching of the Catholic Church. In the Compendium it says, "Because of the communion of saints, the faithful who are still pilgrims on earth are able to help the souls in purgatory by offering prayers in suffrage for them, especially the Eucharistic sacrifice. They also help them by *almsgiving*, indulgences, and works of penance (italics added).[29]"

That summary makes it clear that the Catholic Church is allowing people to have their time in purgatory shortened if their friends and family will give the church money (almsgiving). Like the faith healer on TV that will only heal your arthritis if you are willing to pull out the checkbook, the Catholic Church will only fast-forward the flames of purgatory if you ante up. The prosperity prophets tell you to plant a seed offering for your own good, and the pope is telling to you offer indulgences for the good of the deceased. Both are just taking advantage of people in a time of weakness.

This idea of manipulating indulgences was Martin Luther's lead off point in his famed Ninety-five Theses, which he discreetly nailed to the door of the Catholic Church. And yet as recently as 2005 the *Compendium of the Catechism of the Catholic Church* stated that almsgiving and indulgences were the duty of the living in light of the dead.

In conclusion to this chapter, Jesus did not go to purgatory because purgatory is not a real place. Even if it were, there was no sin, whether mortal or venial, found in Christ. What is more important for the reader to know is that purgatory is not an option for anyone today either.

---

[29]   *Compendium of the Catechism of the Catholic Church*, p.210-211

Each person must make sure that he is right with Christ today, for after death it is too late to do anything about it. No well meaning relative can better your situation for you, whether now or in the next life. Do whatever it takes to be right with God today.